SOUTHERN ENGLAND

WITH COLOURMASTER

SOUTHERN ENGLAND

WITH
COLOURMASTER

Published by Colourmaster International
Caxton Road, St. Ives, Huntingdon, England

FIRST PUBLISHED 1972

PUBLISHED BY COLOURMASTER INTERNATIONAL
PRINTED IN GREAT BRITAIN BY PHOTO PRECISION LTD., ST. IVES, HUNTINGDON
ISBN 0 85933 007 9

INTRODUCTION

We have taken Southern England to comprise Kent, Sussex and Hampshire (including the Isle of Wight). Within this area there is an almost endless variety of unspoiled natural beauty, both inland and along the coast. Here also are cathedrals and churches, stately homes and humble cottages that span the centuries and write our history in stone. Kent, variously known as the Garden of England, the Birthplace of our Christianity and the Gateway to England. Sussex, so typically English that it has been said that Sussex *is* England. Hampshire, whose county town was old before the Romans came. Visitors either with or without specialized interests will find much to occupy their time and attention in Southern England but it is hoped that residents also will find something in the text and illustrations to deepen their affection for the area.

On the map, Kent fills roughly an inverted triangle, each side having its special character. The north shore, continuing the line of the river Thames, is mostly low-lying or with cliffs of clay and shingly beaches. On the south-east side the chalk cliffs of Thanet and Dover and Folkestone are interspersed with low beaches of shingle and marvellous sands along by Dymchurch. On the south-west Kent merges with Surrey and Sussex in a wonderland of luxuriant hills and valleys and delightful farm cottages and historic homes.

Sussex is divided for administration purposes into East Sussex, with a charming old world principal town at Lewes, and West Sussex which has the cathedral city of Chichester as its capital. The county is proud of its extensive and varied coast line and equally proud of its charming inland scenery among the downs, the sandstone hills and the weald. Here is an abundance of lovely villages, churches and inns and for good measure, castles and country mansions, heaths and commons and rivers which cleave attractive valleys through the hills.

As for Hampshire, one of England's largest counties, it is interesting that in paleolithic days what is now the Isle of Wight was then part of the mainland. Winchester, in Roman times, was Venta Belgarum, and before that it was called Caergwent. Large areas of Hampshire are still unspoiled, with all the gentle beauty of downs, heaths and chalk streams and the last of England's great forests.

Romsey, Portsmouth and Southampton have played their parts in English history while at Selbourne there lived and died in the eighteenth century someone to whom lovers of natural history owe a debt of gratitude that can never be repaid.

As with the other books in this series, the emphasis has been placed on high quality illustrations in both colour and black and white, with the addition of relatively short captions of a mainly factual nature because the pictures selected can speak for themselves.

The Pantiles, Royal Tunbridge Wells, Kent.

The town's reputation was established early in the 17th century when Lord North discovered the medicinal qualities of a chalybeate well he had noticed there. It soon became fashionable for Royalty and the court to take the waters and visits were paid by Queen Henrietta Maria, wife of Charles I, by Charles II and his Queen, by the Duke of York (later James II) and by Princess Anne (later Queen Anne), by which time paved walks and rows of trees had appeared and the Pantiles had begun to take shape. Beau Nash was installed as Master of Ceremonies in 1735 and he soon introduced the gaming rooms and lotteries, balls and concerts that made Tunbridge Wells popular with the fashionable set. By the advent of the Victorian era the town was developing into more of a residential resort and in 1909, during the reign of Edward VII, the prefix Royal was authorised. The Pantiles retain much of their ancient charm to this day and one can still take the famous waters.

Knole House, Sevenoaks, Kent.

Knole, one of the largest private houses in England, is situated at the Tonbridge end of the pleasant market town of Sevenoaks just to the east of A21 about 25 miles from London. The mansion dates mainly from the 15th century and has a Jacobean interior with a fine collection of both 17th and 18th century furniture. Set in a 1000 acres park, Knole has been the home of the Sackville family for 350 years. In 1946 the house was handed over to the National Trust who open it to the public at advertised times.

The Rock Gardens at Westgate-on-Sea, Kent.

The north-east corner of Kent which lies on the seaward side of the rivers Stour and Wantsun is known as the Isle of Thanet and includes the popular resorts of Broadstairs, Margate and Ramsgate.

Margate likes to describe itself as five resorts in one because the borough of Margate's nine mile foreshore also includes Cliftonville, Westbrook, Westgate-on-Sea and Birchington. In all there are 300 acres of parks and gardens and within them something like a quarter of a million flowering plants are grown each year. During the spring and summer months in particular their superbly colourful displays are greatly appreciated.

Tonbridge Castle, Kent.

As can be seen, there are now only the slight but picturesque remains of Tonbridge castle, which was built near the north bank of the river Medway and is old enough to remember having been besieged by William Rufus. At the other end of the High Street, near the junction of A21 and A227 is Tonbridge School for boys, founded in 1553.

Dane Park Lake, Cliftonville, Kent.

Here is another example, this time illustrated in colour, of the charm of the parks and gardens for which the borough of Margate is so deservedly well-known. Shady trees, flowering shrubs, bedding plants and the placid waters of the lake all contribute to this pleasing little composition.

Margate is 74 miles from London with which it is connected by good roads and all electric express trains. During the summer months there is also a popular steamer service from the Tower of London pier.

The North Foreland Lighthouse, Kent.

The importance of lighthouses as aids to safe navigation at sea has been recognized from earliest times and it will not escape recollection that the Pharos of Alexandria is one of the Seven Wonders of the World. The Corporation of Trinity House is the principal lighthouse and pilotage authority for the United Kingdom and was active even before Henry VIII granted the Corporation its first charter in 1514.

The North Foreland lighthouse is situated on the north-east corner of the Kent coast between Margate and Broadstairs. It is claimed that there was a candlelit lighthouse on the North Foreland as long ago as 1505. There was certainly a coal fire light there in 1634. In 1790 the tower height was raised to 64 feet 7 inches, and oil lamps with reflectors and lenses replaced the open coal fire. Electric filament lamps were installed in 1930 giving a light range of up to 21 miles. The height of the light above sea level is 188 feet. The lighthouse was scheduled as a building of special architectural or historical interest in 1950.

The Royal Harbour entrance, Ramsgate, Kent.

Ramsgate's commodious harbour can accommodate large numbers of sailing and other types of pleasure and fishing craft. There is a small dry dock and slipway and close by are the coastguard and lifeboat stations. Ramsgate is about 3 miles south of Broadstairs, which has many associations with Charles Dickens, and is about 5 miles southeast of Margate. A popular resort with splendid sands and promenades, it was the base and starting point for the first cross-Channel hovercraft service which was begun in 1966. Within the town is the magnificent St. Augustine's Abbey Roman Catholic church which was designed by Augustus Pugin, the celebrated 19th century architect, and regarded by many discerning authorities as his masterpiece. Other examples of his work can be seen in the Houses of Parliament in London.

The Friars, Aylesford, Kent.

The Friars is the name of a Carmelite priory whose association with Aylesford dates back to 1242. Dispossessed during the Reformation, the Carmelites did not return until 1949. Since 1949 miracles of restoration and addition have been wrought with great skill and devotion. Pilgrimages to the Friars are frequently made not only by Roman Catholics but also by Anglican and other Christian denominations. Accommodation at the Guest House is available for men and women and there are facilities for religious conferences and retreats.

Those who appreciate things of beauty will find a great deal to interest them at the Friars. The skill of the masons who worked the Kentish ragstone, the inspiration behind Kossowski's magnificent ceramics, stained glass by that distinguished artist Moira Forsyth, Michael Clark's great statue of the Glorious Virgin of the Assumption, fine paintings and wrought iron work are but some of the pleasures in store for the visitor.

Aylesford is about 30 miles from London. There are electric train services from London to Aylesford and to Maidstone. By road the Friars can be reached by the A20 to Ditton and then turn left or by M2 as far as the Chatham and Maidstone exit (A229) turning right off A229 at the Lower Bell Inn.

The Viking Ship, Pegwell Bay, Kent.

This is a full size model of the kind of Viking ship that brought Hengist and Horsa to England in A.D. 449. The coast from Ramsgate to Deal is of great historical interest because it was along here that both the Roman landings were made and here also that St. Augustine landed in A.D. 597 bringing his Christian message from Rome.

The Weavers, Canterbury, Kent.

These lovely old houses, overlooking a branch of the river Stour, are a reminder of the days when Huguenot refugees from religious persecution came over and settled in this country, bringing their valuable skills with them. Their descendants still use a chapel set aside for them in Canterbury Cathedral. Considering that almost one-third of Canterbury was destroyed by bombs during World War II it is quite remarkable that so much of historical, architectural and ecclesiastical interest was spared.

Canterbury Cathedral, Kent.

Built on land originally given to St. Augustine by King Ethelbert, the present cathedral is basically Norman but the nave belongs to the 14th century and the Bell Harry Tower to the 15th century. After Archbishop Thomas à Becket was murdered in the northwest transept in 1170 thousands of pilgrims visited his tomb until the martyr's shrine was destroyed by Henry VIII. The Norman crypt, the largest in the world, is of outstanding interest, as also are the 12th century choir, the medieval glass and the Black Prince's tomb.

The Westgate, Canterbury, Kent.

While the cathedral must always be its main feature, Canterbury is a fascinating city in its own right. Called Durovernum by the Romans, there is still much interesting evidence of their occupation. Sections of the medieval city walls are to be seen and the sole surviving city gate, called the Westgate and illustrated opposite, is a spectacular 14th century structure created during the reign of Edward III.

Canterbury Cathedral through the King's School archway.

The twin western towers and part of the roof of the nave of the cathedral are here seen framed through the King's School archway. The King's School, one of the oldest foundations in the country, possesses a unique feature in the form of a Norman external staircase. The cathedral nave is of 14th century date and a series of steps had to be constructed to connect it with the choir and apse which are two hundred years older, having been designed by William de Sens after the fire of 1174. The tomb of the Black Prince, son of Edward III, who died in 1376, is in the Trinity Chapel. There is some exceptionally fine medieval stained glass in a number of the cathedral windows while the huge Norman crypt contains the Chapel of Our Lady.

Dover Castle, Kent.

Dover, chief of the Cinque Ports, was a port in the days of the Romans. The castle dates from Norman times and the huge, square keep was built between 1181 and 1187 by Henry II. It measures 98 feet by 96 feet at ground level, where the walls are 22 feet thick. The tops of the turrets are 95 feet high. The keep was protected by an inner line of ramparts and towers, and an outer line was added during the thirteenth century containing the Constable's Tower at the main entrance. In the period 1179 to 1191 records show a total of nearly £700 was spent on work on the Castle, probably under the supervision of a certain "Maurice the Engineer."

The White Cliffs of Dover.

The white cliffs of Dover have been full of meaning to thousands of people over the years. To some they have meant home, to other safety from persecution and injustice. To Bleriot or to a cross Channel swimmer they have brought an objective into sight and in World War II they represented to the enemy what proved to be an unachievable ambition.

St. Margaret's Bay, Kent.

This view looks down from the top of the chalk cliffs to the small, secluded beach at St. Margaret's Bay which is between Dover and Deal and close to the South Foreland. The cliffs, which are such a dominant feature of this part of the Kent coast, reach a height of more than four hundred feet in places. The little village above the bay is known as St. Margaret-at-Cliffe. It has a quite magnificent church with richly decorated stone carving and a battlemented tower. Adjoining the village is a fine granite memorial erected to the memory of the men who formed the Dover Patrol during the first World War.

A little further northward up the coast is Walmer Castle, one of the several Kent castles built by Henry VIII. It is now the official residence of the Lord Warden of the Cinque Ports, a sinecure office bestowed only on very famous men. Dover is the chief of the Cinque Ports, the others being Hastings, Sandwich, Romney and Hythe. These ports—more important in some cases then than they are now—combined as early as the 13th century to defend this vulnerable part of the country against raiders from across the English Channel. For the historically minded visitor there is a wealth of interest in each of them.

Kingsnorth Gardens, Folkestone, Kent.

The road which climbs out of Dover towards Folkestone presents a magnificent panorama extending over Folkestone and far beyond, by Romney Marsh to Dungeness.

A popular yet unspoiled seaside resort, Folkestone is also an important cross-Channel port handling a million passengers a year. Five miles of sea front extend from the Warren to the delightful suburb of Sandgate. The town itself consists of an old part near the harbour and a larger, modern part to the west which is tree-lined and spacious. Folkestone's unique feature, however, is the broad mile-long cliff-top promenade called The Leas, with beautiful lawns and well kept flower beds from which winding paths drop down to the beach nearly two hundred feet below.

Parks and open spaces are plentiful in Folkestone. Kingsnorth Gardens, half a mile behind the sea front, contain a fascinating display of flowers and shrubs, immaculate lawns and lily-ponds artistically laid out in Italian style to make a quite enchanting composition. From dusk during the summer months the gardens are floodlit.

The Zig-Zag Path, Folkestone, Kent.

Starting on The Leas near the bandstand, the Zig-Zag Path slopes sharply to the beach between rockeries filled with colourful plants and shrubs of many varieties which visitors can enjoy as they pass or from the seats which are spaced out all the way down.

In contrast to the orderly exhibits of flowers and shrubs which abound in Folkestone are those less sophisticated displays of natural beauty to be seen at the Warren, beyond the East Cliff. This is an area of tremendous interest to nature lovers for here is a profusion of wild flowers growing among the trees and shrubs of what has been described as a great natural garden. Grassy banks and winding paths put the finishing touches to a splendid sight.

Dungeness Lighthouse, Kent.

The Dungeness promontory lies between Rye and Littlestone-on-Sea. About five miles inland is Lydd airport.

Soon after 1600 Trinity House reported against a proposal for a light at Dungeness Point but persistence by the petitioner met with success. Trinity House withdrew its opposition and Sir Edward Howard received a patent in August 1615 and marked the spot by an open coal fire. Navigators recognised its value immediately. For its maintenance the patent authorised the levy of dues on shipping for a period of forty years. This appears to be the first British lighthouse erected solely for the benefit of general coastal navigation.

Although a tower with a coal fire on top had been built nearer to the sea in 1635 the sea had again receded so much by 1746 that the light had become misleading. Samuel Wyatt built a new tower one hundred and sixteen feet high in 1792 which lasted for over a century. In 1862 electricity replaced oil as the illuminant and the tower was painted black with a white band to make it more conspicuous by day. The further recession of the sea necessitated yet another lighthouse which was completed in 1904. Fifty years later the light became obscured by the erection of a nuclear power station and another—the present—lighthouse had to be built. Brought into operation in 1961 it was built of pre-cast concrete rings each five feet high, six inches thick and twelve feet in diameter, fitted one above the other and painted in black and white bands impregnated into the concrete. The tower rises one hundred and forty feet from a spiral concrete ramp. The high pressure Xenon electric arc lamp has a range of twenty three miles. Although capable of automatic operation, the lighthouse is manned by a Principal Keeper and two Assistant Keepers.

Bodiam Castle, Sussex.

Bodiam Castle is in East Sussex, close to the Kent county boundary three miles south of Hawkhurst. It was built towards the end of the 14th century as a stronghold when the river Rother was navigable to French marauders who might have attempted an assault. The exterior with towers over sixty feet high is in a remarkably fine state of preservation. The interior is in ruins but it is possible to trace the position of the well arranged hall, chapel, staterooms, kitchen and retainers quarters.

Hastings Castle, Sussex.

The ruins shown in the picture opposite are all that now remains of Hastings Castle. It dates back to Norman times, having been built on West Hill to protect what was then an important harbour as well as to resist any possibility of attack from the landward side. Hastings, it will be remembered, was one of the original Cinque Ports—the only one of the five to be located in the county of Sussex.

Old Cottages at Winchelsea, Sussex.

This fascinating little town has a long and interesting history. Rebuilt after the old town had been submerged by the sea in the 13th century it is a pleasant example of early town planning. There are many well preserved buildings in a setting of trees and open spaces and some of the old gateways, notably Strand Gate, still survive. The town was sacked three times by the French in the 14th century.

The Beach at St. Leonards, Sussex.

St. Leonards is contiguous with Hastings and together they form a County Borough and one of the most progressive and popular seaside resorts in the county. There are fine long double promenades and splendid gardens, a shingle beach with sand at low tide, an Olympic swimming pool and a comprehensive range of hotel and other types of holiday accommodation.

The Fishing fleet, Hastings, Sussex.

Hastings is still noted for its small fishing fleet which operates from the Stade in the old town below Castle Hill at the eastern end of the promenade. Stade is an old Saxon word meaning landing place. The old town is a fascinating collection of narrow streets and quaint passages with ancient timbered and clap-boarded buildings that have survived the centuries.

Beachy Head Lighthouse, Eastbourne, Sussex.

Beachy Head lighthouse, completed in 1902, replaced one which had been built on the headland in 1828. Because of its height above sea level the earlier light, in certain mist and fog conditions, became invisible to mariners. The present lighthouse is 153 feet high over all. The base is 47 feet in diameter and the tower is solid for the first 48 feet apart from a space for storing drinking water. The incandescent oil light, of 274,000 candelas, has a range of up to 24 miles.

The De La Warr Pavilion, Bexhill-on-Sea, Sussex.

Bexhill-on-Sea lies between Eastbourne and Hastings. It is a modern resort on an attractive part of the Sussex coast with downs and woodlands immediately inland. The magnificent De La Warr Pavilion is the entertainment centre par excellence. It contains a 1200 seat theatre, a restaurant, a cafeteria, a ballroom, a balcony overlooking the splendid terrace and a flat sun roof over the whole of the east wing. It is owned and managed by the Corporation.

Splash Point, Seaford, Sussex.

All parts of Seaford, a small resort between Newhaven and Eastbourne, are close either to the sea or to the rolling South Downs and here, at Splash Point, just beyond the eastern end of the promenade, they meet. Some of the most interesting and exhilarating walks in the whole of the county can be made from Seaford, including visits to Alfriston, Cuckmere Haven and the Long Man of Wilmington.

A Downs Ranger, Eastbourne, Sussex.

The glorious, rolling expanse of the chalky South Downs, which eventually tipple five hundred feet into the sea at Beachy Head, begin near Petersfield in Hampshire. They are wooded in the west with bare grassland in the east. There is a Bridleway running 80 miles from Alfriston, through Eastbourne to Buriton in Hampshire. Nearly four hundred square miles of the South Downs have been officially designated as an area of outstanding natural beauty.

Keere Street, Lewes, Sussex.

The county town of Lewes, in a gap in the South Downs carved out by the river Ouse, is overlooked by hills which rise to five and six hundred feet—Mount Harry, to the west, is 639 feet above sea level.

The ruined castle dominates the town and is an ideal place from which to obtain views in every direction. Lewes lives history, far more than can be mentioned here, but suffice it to say that the Museum, the old Priory, several ancient churches, Anne of Cleve's house, and the many byways are but samples of the riches to be found huddled together in this lovely town. Take a look at Keere Street, off the High Street, and you will marvel at the foolhardiness of the Prince Regent who, for a wager, drove a coach and four down its narrow cobbled steep incline.

The Lawns from the Wish Tower, Eastbourne, Sussex.

Beachy Head and the downs have already been mentioned in the Eastbourne context but the reference here is to Eastbourne itself, a clean, orderly and important resort first popularized as a result of the visit of four of George III's children in 1780 "to a watering place of great respectability." Beautifully kept parks and gardens, three miles of promenade and concert halls with a reputation for good music help to make Eastbourne popular with visitors all the year round.

The Barbican, Lewes, Sussex.

The massive barbican, of early 14th century date, was built as an outer defence to the castle which had already been built by the Normans and which, today, is scheduled as an Ancient Monument. St. Anne's church and St. John's church also have Norman origins and in the latter is the tomb of William the Conqueror's daughter Gundrada.

The Harbour entrance, Newhaven, Sussex.

Our illustration shows one of the fleet of cross-Channel steamers which maintain regular and frequent car and passenger ferry links between Newhaven and Dieppe, a service run jointly by British Rail and French National Railways. The long breakwater affords an excellent vantage point from which to view the harbour's many activities. In addition to the cross-Channel packets, there is usually a busy assortment of cargo vessels, yachts, launches and fishing boats to engage one's attention. From the lighthouse at the end of the harbour wall there is a good view across the water to Seaford and Seaford Head.

Tudor Cottages, Rottingdean, Sussex.

The village of Rottingdean, about three miles from Brighton, straddles the fine coast road (A259) that links Brighton with Newhaven and Eastbourne. It can also be reached most enjoyably on foot from Brighton along the undercliff walk that has been built between the base of the chalk cliffs and the beach. On the inland side of the main road Rottingdean has retained a great deal of charm, with a pretty little pond, flint and timber houses and cottages and the delightful St. Margaret's church with windows by Sir Edward Burne-Jones, the celebrated Victorian artist whose remains are buried in the churchyard. Rudyard Kipling, a nephew of Burne-Jones, lived for some time in Rottingdean at Elm House which is on the north side of The Green. On the seaward side of the main road Rottingdean has its own little promenade, swimming pool, shops and restaurants.

Lindfield Pond, Haywards Heath, Sussex.

Its pleasant situation and good electric railway links with London and Brighton have made Haywards Heath a much sought after residential area. The placid pond in the black and white illustration is named Lindfield Pond, Lindfield being a neighbouring and extremely picturesque village of fine old houses. At Heaselands and at Borde Hill, each on the outskirts of Haywards Heath are some very lovely gardens open to the public at advertised times.

A night view of the old Steine Fountain, Brighton, Sussex.

Brighton has something of the order of a thousand acres of parks and gardens. The Valley Gardens (Old Steine and London Road), including the fountain shown in the colour illustration on the opposite page, are impressively illuminated at night to add still further to the many attractions of what to many people is England's premier resort.

The Ypres Tower, Rye, Sussex.

Rye, on the river Rother, is a fascinating little town of considerable historical and architectural interest and importance. From Norman times through to the 16th century it was a busy port but today the sea is two miles away. The 13th century Mermaid Inn was once a hive of smuggling activity, the church contains much good Norman work and the Ypres Tower which changed hands as long ago as 1430, was once a prison. Every nook and cranny of Rye demands to be explored and photographed.

The University of Sussex, Brighton.

The severely modern architectural style of the University of Sussex contrasts sharply with, for example, the extravagance of the design of the Royal Pavilion. Founded in 1961 the building is situated on the outskirts of Brighton close to Stanmer Park off the Lewes road. There are about four thousand full time students.

The Lanes, Brighton, Sussex.

The attractive series of byways known as the Lanes contrast piquantly with Brighton's spacious Regency squares. Originally the bow-windowed 17th century cottages of the fishing families of old Brighton, they have been adapted to form a fascinating pedestrian precinct specializing in antique, souvenir and curio shops which are popular with collectors from all over the world on account of the quality and variety of the articles displayed for sale. The Lanes are within the area bounded by Kings Road, West Street, East Street and North Street and adjoin Brighton Square.

The Royal Pavilion, Brighton, Sussex.

When George, Prince of Wales, became Prince Regent in 1812 he engaged John Nash to re-design his Brighton house on the lines of a Mogul's palace, with domes and pinnacles and minarets in the eastern style which we see today. The Royal Pavilion, which is magnificently furnished and includes pieces on loan from Buckingham Palace, is open daily to the public.

Heene Terrace, Worthing, Sussex.

Heene Terrace, less than a mile to the west of Worthing pier, is just off the Marine Parade. Its trim lawns and well kept flower beds are typical features of this popular seaside holiday and residential town, second in size in Sussex only to Brighton and Hove. It has five miles of sea-front, an all the year round municipal orchestra, three golf courses, good shops and easy access to some splendid inland countryside.

Marina Gardens, Littlehampton, Sussex.

Littlehampton is between Worthing and Bognor Regis. You can follow the sequence of beaches from Worthing successively through Goring, Ferring, Angmering and Rustington to Littlehampton which nestles by the side of the fast flowing river Arun. Largely modern in its appearance, Littlehampton is, in fact, quite an old centre of habitation which drew its living from the sea and the river. It is a paradise for children. Apart from the amusements provided for them, the Green, between the road and the promenade, makes a safe playground in addition to the beach. The illustrated expanse of exquisitely kept gardens is situated almost equidistantly between the river and the sea front promenade.

The Pier and Lighthouse, Littlehampton, Sussex.

The river Arun is a valuable asset to visitors to Littlehampton because it enables them to take delightful trips up river to Arundel, Amberley and Burham, involving journeys of seven, fourteen and ten miles respectively. Boat trips along the coast or for sea fishing are also, of course, available from the quay. It is claimed with every justification that few other resorts can provide so compactly the varied charms of sea, river and countryside that Littlehampton has to offer and these considerable attractions are appreciated by residents and visitors alike.

The Cathedral and Bishop's Palace, Chichester, Sussex.

This is a view from the forecourt of the Bishop's Palace. Only the buildings on the left hand side of the photograph are now used by the Bishop; those on the right are used by the Prebendal School. The gateway to the Palace is 14th century and the chapel and kitchens date back to the 13th century. A brief description of the Cathedral will be found on page 64.

The Market Cross, Chichester, Sussex.

The cross is situated at the intersection of what were originally Roman roads. Built very early in the 16th century by Bishop Storey, it was erected to shelter traders who came into town to sell their wares. Complete with flying buttresses, it is one of the most elaborate market crosses in the country. Chichester possesses many other architectural treasures which include not only the magnificent cathedral but also some quite superb Georgian town houses.

Chichester Cathedral from St. Richard's Walk.

St. Richard's Walk is the name given to the path from the cloisters to the Close and, as can be seen, it provides an opportunity to appreciate the steepled tower which comprises the central external feature of this lovely cathedral. The see of Chichester was established by the Normans in 1075 and it was Bishop de Luffa, who was consecrated in 1091, who began to build the cathedral. Consecrated in 1184 and seriously damaged by fire three years later, much of it is in the Norman style of architecture. The retrochoir, behind the High Altar, is a little later, representing the transitional period and the use of pointed instead of rounded arches. The spire above the central tower collapsed in 1861 and was rebuilt under Sir Gilbert Scott's supervision. The Bell Tower, 15th century, is the only separate cathedral bell tower in England.

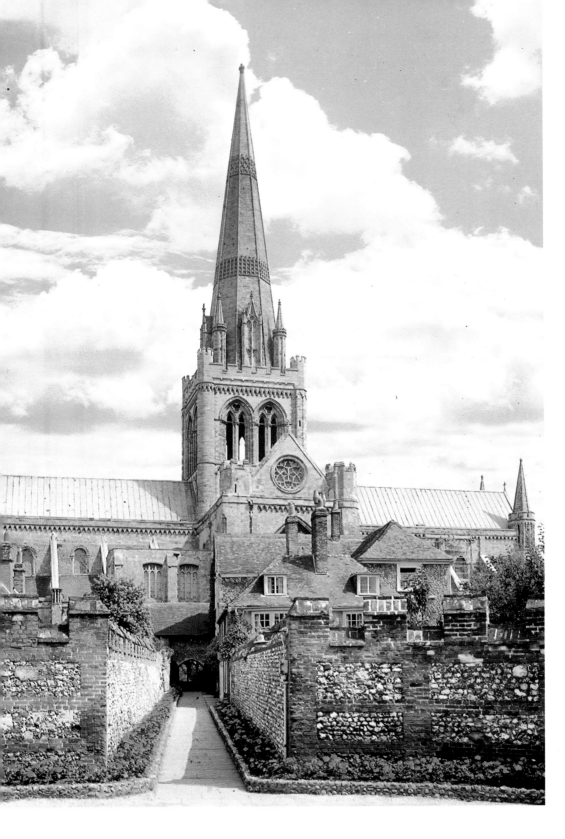

The Countryside near Petersfield, Hampshire.

Petersfield, with its lovely Georgian and other period houses, was an important stage on the London—Portsmouth road in the old coaching days. The old church and the spacious market square are other interesting features of what is still the principal town in this part of east Hampshire. The surrounding countryside reveals a greater variety of attractive scenery than might perhaps have been expected. Heathland, downland, tree clad hills, some of which can attain six and seven hundred feet or more in height, and a patchwork of meadows and cornfields contribute harmoniously to the visitor's enjoyment of some still largely unspoiled scenery.

Winchester Cathedral, Hampshire.

Winchester, in the vale of the river Itchen, was an important settlement even before the Romans built a town there. It became Alfred's capital when he became King of Wessex in 871 and it continued to be of great importance after the Norman conquest. The present cathedral, which replaced an earlier Saxon church, was begun in 1079 by Bishop Wakelin and the most interesting Norman work to be seen today is in the transepts. Big changes were made in the 14th century, especially by Bishop William of Wykeham, who gave the nave the pointed arches and early fan vaulting typical of the early perpendicular style of architecture. The cathedral eventually achieved a length of 556 feet which made it at one time the longest cathedral in Europe. Its very many treasures include the 12th century Tournai marble font, the 14th century carved misericords, the 15th century reredos and several magnificent chantry chapels, while in the library are priceless books and manuscripts which include a copy of Bede's history and a superbly illuminated 13th century bible.

Winchester College, one of England's oldest public schools, was founded by William of Wykeham in 1382 and its buildings now span a period of almost six hundred years. Visitors to the city will also wish to see the King Alfred statue and Hyde Abbey, where Alfred is thought to have been buried, the 13th century Great Hall of the old castle and, a mile outside the city, the Hospital of St. Cross with its Norman church and 15th century buildings—one of the oldest charitable institutions in the world.

The Windmill, Bembridge, Isle of Wight.

The remaining illustrations in this publication are devoted to the Isle of Wight, administratively part of Hampshire and known to the Romans as Vectis. A mere twenty two miles by thirteen, to some people it is England in miniature, with its seaside edge, its downs and glens, cliffs and beaches, farms and cottages, churches and castles and stately homes. There is certainly a great deal on the island that awaits your pleasure.

Bembridge, whose beautifully restored old windmill, built in 1700, is illustrated opposite, is on the south side of the estuary of the river Yar. With a safe anchorage for small yachts, it is the headquarters of a well-known sailing club, it has good sands and bathing, a small public school that has a fine library of Ruskin's works and also at Bembridge is an amusing piece of tavern architecture in the shape of the Pilot Boat Inn.

Thatched Cottages at Brighstone, Isle of Wight.

A short distance inland from the south-west coast, Brighstone's thatched cottages, with their little flower gardens almost spilling over into the road, are an attractive sight. The intriguing small medieval church, much restored, sent three of its rectors to become bishops, including the saintly Bishop Ken, the famous hymn-writer.

Scene at Cowes, Isle of Wight.

Cowes is on the north coast facing the Solent. There are two communities, West Cowes and East Cowes, situated on either side of the Medina estuary. The first is the mecca of those who are addicted to sailing. Here is the headquarters of the Royal Yacht Squadron, founded in 1815 and the only yacht club that is permitted to fly the white ensign. The great regatta in the first week of August, "Cowes Week," is a tremendously fashionable event. Royal patronage has been extended to Cowes since the time of the Prince Regent, who later became George IV.

St. Blasius Church, Shanklin, Isle of Wight.

Shanklin, in the south-east of the island, is situated between Sandown and Ventnor. The much restored church of St. Blasius is at the foot of Shanklin Down. Old Shanklin, with its thatched cottages and glorious gardens, the tree and fern clad Chine which winds down to the sea, the pier and glorious sands are the outstanding features of this sun-blessed resort.

Godshill, Isle of Wight.

Godshill, about four miles inland west of Shanklin, is an almost wilfully pretty village. Its church, mainly 14th century on earlier foundations, contains some finely carved tombs and many monuments to members of the Worsley family whose home at one time was at Appledurrombe House about two miles away and now in ruins in a mournful park.

St. Boniface Church, Bonchurch, Isle of Wight.

Bonchurch now forms part of Ventnor, at the eastern end of the south coast. The old church of St. Boniface, which contains some Norman work, was built on the site of an even earlier church. St. Boniface was a missionary from Devon who was martyred in Germany. The decorative pond adjoining the village street was a gift from H. de Vere Stacpoole, the novelist, who is buried at Bonchurch.

Winkle Street, Calbourne, Isle of Wight.

Calbourne is some four miles from Carisbrooke Castle and five miles from the south-west coast. The rose and clematis clad cottages of Winkle Street, some with thatched and some with tiled roofs, are perfectly charming and richly deserve their popularity with visitors to the island.

Freshwater Bay, Isle of Wight.

Freshwater Bay is about three miles east of the Needles and lies below the high chalk cliffs which mark the end of Tennyson Down, so named after the poet-laureate who came to Freshwater in 1853 to live at Farringford House. The isolated sea-girt rocks in our illustration are known as the Arch and the Stag.

The Needles, Isle of Wight.

At the south-western tip of the island are The Needles, three colossal molars of chalk rising from the sea, and at the end of them is the Needles Lighthouse built in 1859. The tower is 109 feet high and is built of granite. The light is visible for a distance of seventeen miles. South of the Needles is Scratchell's Bay whose high, rugged cliffs are the haunt of sea birds.

The Car Ferry Quay, Yarmouth, Isle of Wight.

Yarmouth, with its excellent harbour, is on the north coast and faces Lymington, with which it has a car ferry connection. It is perhaps the most picturesque and certainly, after Newport, the most historic town on the island. The castle, adjoining the harbour jetty, was built by Henry VIII. There is a little square, there are narrow, salty streets and there are several old inns of great charm and character.

Alum Bay, Isle of Wight.

Alum Bay, on the north side of The Needles, is especially popular on account of its re-markable, multi-coloured sandy cliffs. There is said to be a range of twenty one colours altogether and glass phials of the different sands are sold as souvenirs. The colours in the cliffs are at their brightest after rain.

The Old Village, Shanklin, Isle of Wight.

The black and white illustration shows some of the beautifully preserved thatched cottages in the Old Village of Shanklin. Near the lovely little Crab Hotel is a fountain on which are inscribed verses written by Longfellow when he visited Shanklin more than a hundred years ago.

Whippingham Church, Isle of Wight.

Adjacent to Osborne House, once the country home of Queen Victoria, is Whippingham Church which was largely designed by the Prince Consort. Built in 1849 it, became their place of public worship. It contains many ornate Royal Family memorials and the present marble reredos is a memorial to Queen Victoria herself. The lych gate in the foreground of our illustration is made of Indian teak wood.

Index to Illustrations